Honor the wisdom of the heart.

—PROVERB

To mom with love
on Mother's Day 2012.

Love, Robin

MOTHERHOOD:

All love begins and ends there.

—ROBERT BROWNING

DEAR MOM

TEXT by Dan Zadra
DESIGN by Lianne Onart

favorite memories

Your home is where your favorite memories are.

—PIETER-DIRK UYS

MOTHERHOOD

It's one of the world's most demanding and creative jobs.
The days are long, sometimes extending all through the
night. It requires a wise mind, a patient hand, and a caring
heart. It involves leadership, organization, transportation,
entertainment, psychology, and lots of intuition. Anyone
who can handle all this, and do it year after year with
a smile in her eyes and love in her heart, has to be somebody
pretty special. She is.

home

...HOME

      that our feet may leave,
but not our hearts.

—OLIVER WENDELL HOLMES

Mother—that was the bank
where we deposited
all our hurts and worries.

—T. DEWITT TALMAGE

Who ran to help me when I fell,
And would some pretty story tell,
Or kiss the place to make it well?

My mother.

—ANN TAYLOR

A MOTHER

laughs our laughter,
sheds our tears,
returns our love,
fears our fears.

She lives our joys,
cares our cares,
and all our hopes and
dreams she shares.

—JULIA SUMMERS

she lives our joys

WHATEVER ELSE is unsure in this...world,
a mother's love is not.

—JAMES JOYCE

A MOTHER IS A PERSON

who, seeing there are only four pieces
of pie for five people, promptly
announces she never did care for pie.

—TENNEVA JORDAN

When you thought I wasn't looking,
I felt you kiss me goodnight,

AND I FELT LOVED.

—UNKNOWN

loved

BEING A PARENT

means never having a minute...
yet always making a moment.

—MICHAEL NOLAN

an island
of light

...SHE BECAME FOR ME

an island of light, fun, wisdom

where I could run with my
discoveries and torments and
hopes at any time of the day...

—MAY SARTON

SOME OF THE MOST
GLORIOUS DAYS OF CHILDHOOD
are those we spend with our mother in play.

—DALE THOMAS

A heart that loves
is always young.

—GREEK PROVERB

Caring is everything...

—BARON FRIEDRICH VON HÜGEL

If someone listens,

or stretches out a hand,

or whispers a kind word of encouragement,

or attempts to understand...

extraordinary things

begin to happen.

—LORETTA GIRZAITIS

LOVE...was something she lived in action.

—LEO BUSCAGLIA

THROUGH THICK AND THIN,

she kept our house open to hope.

—JOHN KATZER

...a good mother gives her children
a feeling of trust and stability.

She is their earth.
She is the one they can count on
for the things that matter most of all.

—KATHARINE BUTLER HATHAWAY

A mother is the person you need
when absolutely no one else will do.

—PAM BROWN

BIOLOGY

is the least of what
makes someone a mother.

—OPRAH WINFREY

Life is the first gift,
love is the second, and
understanding the third.

—MARGE PIERCY

THE WORD NO

carries a lot more meaning

when spoken by a parent

who also knows how to say yes.

—JOYCE MAYNARD

We didn't always see eye to eye, but we always saw heart to heart.

—UNKNOWN

MOTHERS

are the most instinctive philosophers.

—HARRIET BEECHER STOWE

instinctive

philosophers

A mother understands

what a child does not say.

—JEWISH PROVERB

WHEN I'VE FELT

I could not weather some apparent disaster,
you have stood beside me and told me that I can.

And I have.

—CLARA ORTEGA

SOONER OR LATER

we all quote our mothers.

—BERN WILLIAMS

A MOTHER REJOICES

to see her young ones
strike out on their own,
but she wants to be sure
they've packed a sweater.

—UNKNOWN

CHILDREN AND MOTHERS
never truly part,
bound in the beating of each other's heart.

—CHARLOTTE GRAY

never truly part

MEMORIES

are our greatest inheritance.

—PETER HAMILL

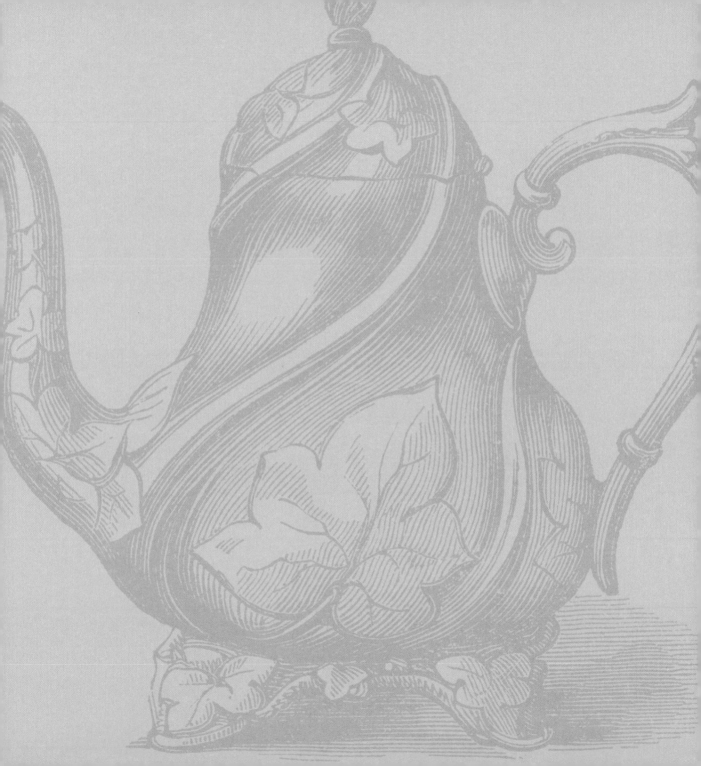

YOUR CHILDREN'S MEMORIES
of home and family will one day become
their bridge to the past,
their shelter in a storm,
and their wings to the future.

—ISABELLA GRAHAM

FOR THIS

I bless you most:

    You give much

    and know not that you give at all.

—KAHLIL GIBRAN

EVERY LITTLE BLESSING

is far too precious to ever forget to say "thank you!"

—LAURA REGIS

I am so glad you are here...
it helps me realize
how beautiful my world is.

—RAINER MARIA RILKE

HOLD TENDERLY

that which you cherish.

—BOB ALBERTI

A MOTHER'S LOVE

is like a circle,
it has no beginning and no ending.

—ART URBAN

no beginni
and n

A MOTHER

holds her children's hands for a while...
their hearts forever.

—UNKNOWN

My mother had a great deal of trouble with me,
but I think she enjoyed it.

—MARK TWAIN

ONLY MOTHERS
   CAN THINK OF THE FUTURE—
   because they give birth to it
   in their children.

   —MAXIM GORKY

The work of your heart,
the work of taking time to listen, to help,
is also your gift to the whole of the world.

—JACK KORNFIELD

Time has a wonderful way

of showing us what REALLY MATTERS.

—MARGARET PETERS

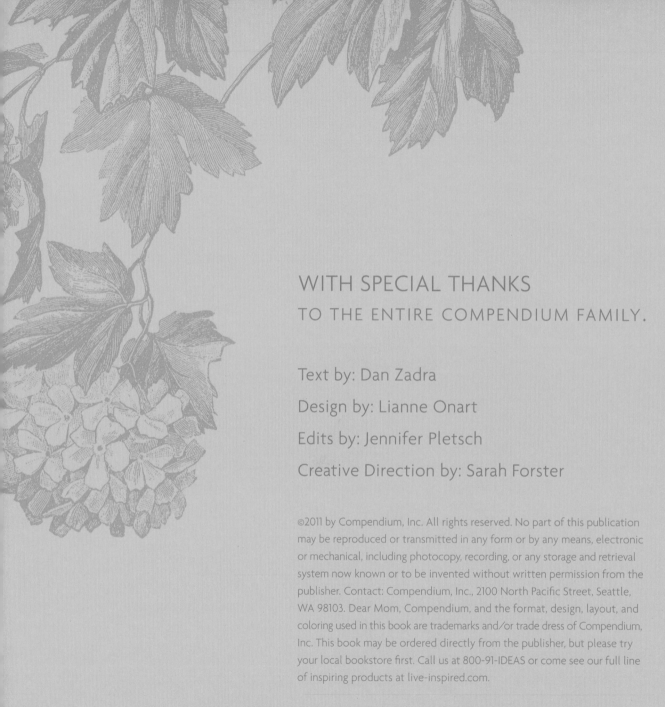

WITH SPECIAL THANKS
TO THE ENTIRE COMPENDIUM FAMILY.

Text by: Dan Zadra

Design by: Lianne Onart

Edits by: Jennifer Pletsch

Creative Direction by: Sarah Forster

1st Printing. Printed in China with soy inks.